Lucifer in the Resthome

Lucifer in the Resthome

Matthew McKay

Plum Branch Press
Harrisburg

The author and publisher wish to thank and acknowledge the following publications which first published some of these poems: *Berkeley Poetry Review* ("Like the Bats"); *California Quarterly* ("Full Moon"); *Cape Rock* ("The Dice"); *Chicago Review* ("Mine of the Lost Oak"); *Chateau Review* ("For Whatever They Could Make"); *Confrontation* ("Whatever Fortune They Can Stand"); *Cutbank* ("Island"); *Epoch* ("At the Fording Place," "John Muir Learned"); *Florida Quarterly* ("Some Kind of Love Poem"); *Hyperion* ("A Song of Otters"); *The Literary Review* ("Switchbacks"); *The Little Magazine* ("Living with Strangers"); *Loon* ("The Valerie Hotel); *Nimrod* ("Miwok Trail," "Parable of the Perfect Fields," "Wawona Hotel"); *The Ohio Journal* ("Lessons"); *Piedmont Literary Review* ("Exactly Twenty Years"); *Remington Review* ("Requiem"); *Wind* ("Bayley's Joy," "Small Monologue"); *Wisconsin Review* ("In a Theater").

Printed by McNaughton & Gunn, USA

ISBN: 0 9702720 0 6

LCCN: 00 092534

Cover design by Marjaneh Talebi
Cover watercolor by Patrick Fanning
Author photograph by Susan Johnson
Text design by Michele Waters

First Edition

Plum Branch Press
P.O. Box 1504
Harrisburg, PA 17110

Contents

Yosemite Poems

To Jude
for giving me a new life

There it was, word for word,
the poem that took the place of the mountain.

—Wallace Stevens

Lucifer in the Resthome

Notes on the Big Bang

> "The expanding universe will be
> very black, very cold, spreading
> into nothing."
> —Nata Bahcall
> Princeton Astrophysicist

We know now
the center is gone,
and the sum of everything that joins
body to body
is an insufficient gravity
to reverse the course of stars.

We know now
that emptiness is a force
pulling at the chords
until a single note is left
traveling out
to where the string goes still.

We know that atoms collect
into shoulders or lips
and then disperse
without memory of the child
carried from room to room
or any kiss.

The dying mountaineer, we've heard,
radioed his wife
as the snow raged around his tent.
And Canadian Geese
after the last shots
circle above a fallen mate.

Awakening sailors hear the crack
splitting the hull
at the speed of sound.
They float together for a while
then disappear
no more than 50 miles from Halifax.

The ship goes down
with every card game
every oath
still ringing in the engine room,
every murmur of the crowd
watching the launch.

It's dark. The tower built
by Lillie Coit in '37
shines in a floodlight.
Inside are the frescoes
of meat packers and pressmen,
the dock strike of '34,

and Clifford Wight's portrait
of a steelworker:
The face young, arms thick & strong,
wrenches and rivet gun ready
in the half-shadows
to make something.

She Wakens in the Middle of Her Life

In her dream she sees smoke rise
through the morning vapors.
She knows the soldiers in a while will come,
turning the village to a white radiance of bone.
But now, early in the day, Cheyenne women can be seen
bending, taking water from Sand Creek.
Their voices stray across the Autumn air.

She wakens in the middle of her life.
It's hot.
For the first time now she knows
anything can happen.

And going to the stall where she keeps her car,
she sends it up to where the hills begin.
Suddenly she steers around a gopher snake
that's lying lazy on the dark asphalt.
She stops to walk the short way back.
The snake, she thinks, is stupid with the heat
and soon will be run over.

It bites her as she flings it in the weeds.
In the car blood starts to well from small
puncture wounds.
She leans back against the cushions.

In a while the tune comes to an end;
a male voice gives the time.

Downstairs at the Oddfellows Columbarium

Full of August, the air.
A piped-in string quartet
on the empty folding seats.
Some hundred years of noonlight
dusting,
torpid and forgetful,
rows of cinerary urns.

All the names of the dead
a weight
without memory or sound
above kneelers of wrought iron:

Chappelas:
>Matching blue urns,
>pictures of her young and lovely;
>the man older, hard,
>wide-brimmed gangster hat,
>water stains on his face

Bacon and *Boggs:*
>Families poured together
>in a strong box
>of the California Stage Co.

Richmond:
>A small red cross, a Star
>of David, one silver mug,
>one blue bottle of perfume,
>the rolled certificate of passage
>on the Queen Elizabeth II

May:
> Next to her cobalt urn,
> a baseball

Ranzulo:
> A waterfall in bronze,
> eagle frozen on a high cliff,
> wings open ready for flight

White:
> Dimestore plastic werewolves

Jackson:
> The heart-shaped porcelain box
> reading, "If you need me, whistle,"
> and the rhinestone whistle

Then a name I knew: *Sofia*
> whose lover
> secretly enjoyed the baths
> and gave him AIDS, who spent
> his last years counseling the sick,
> whose niche contains one
> blood-red Chinese urn.

Rollercoaster

The empty-eye moon
your father watched,
using the thought and color
of breast to cut

his life into her
impassable skin.

It went wrong,
a vow walking late
and beaten up by gangs.
He died that way
still not held,
not speaking to anybody.

Or maybe she loved
but couldn't take his
one legged talk, not ever once
about this, this moment
between them;
and never, she thinks, knew him.

Then here is the emptiness,
the thunderball clacking and falling,
waves seen coming in
through its parallel struts,
a string of red cars grinding up, hot
oil-soaked wood beneath the day moon.
All breakneck, all weathered slam
designed by another age of grief
so one life at a time
forgets.

And at the edge of the first
and highest chute
their arms rise
as if pulled by secret wires
or as a burden given up,
one after another, after
the sleeping and past ones,
after your father and mother whose
arms rose once
before rushing
before rushing down that faithful death.

Conversation Takes a Turn in Ware Shoals

Insects batted the screen.
They'd been laughing about
protesters who questioned
the war,
but the ex-police chief
got red-faced saying
whoever's been there
and still speaks well of it
is lying.

"At the Bulge
we were ordered to retreat,
the Germans coming hard
at this mountain town.
People ran
carrying satchels and children
through a pass,
high rocks on either side,
and I
had the lead tank, the column
depending on maximum speed.
I drove them down,
feeling them fall
under us
all the way out of there."

His wife,
who had never heard the story,
said, "maybe that's why
you've always been so nervous,"
which meant
all the times he'd just
caught flame and beaten her.

Smoke

Getting up,
the air full of voices
of another life,
loud as the leaves
losing hold.

In the dark morning
the perfume
from fires
drifts through the house
like a love that is real

but cannot touch.

Like the Bats

"I will not be false
to you tonight."
—W. S. Merwin

The shot echoes between wet hills.
A raccoon killed at the pool's edge:
His sack drags over roots and quiet dens.
Now I would tell you anything
to be safe.

Words meekly dangle like the bats,
witches turn miles separating our deaths
to laughter and opaque regard.
Here again is night when I needed you
following day when I did not.
The taxidermist searches
through a drawer of brown glass eyes.

Coldwater

Anyplace
the sun sets
silvering the cross-town wires
is Coldwater.

Anywhere
the wind presses
casements and thresholds –
like words

held in the throat –
is Coldwater.
All over town
parlor lights click on

to keep
the furniture from moving,
to tell
the emotional history

of wallpaper.
In Coldwater
glass angels get up
for bed,

bumping each other
with a tinkling sound,
shattering
against steps.

Prostitute in Her Bedroom, Alaska

The cups & spoons, the comfort
of honey on the draped table.
A nineteenth century sun
scalds the mirror
and pinned up cards
next to her bed: The place
where snow cannot fall,
where the blinding white hills
soften into linen & the fox fur
rug. She waits
for them: A rage
sluicing from the mines
and naked tents, only
pausing at the touch
of her shoulder and breast.

Leaving Home

It'll be hot.
Light travels the long way
to touch
the clotheslines and fences,
the still branches of hawthorn,
a woman
turning the dark earth
with a trowel.

The light
flares from the dashboard,
from the white
shoulders of a girl
skimming the sidewalk –
a day doing its damage
where every desire turns
devotion

to a thin, thin porcelain.

Island

The chain drops through transparent bursts of tide;
his anchor rests between the inlets at a full café;
only thin trees come down to violets in a window ledge.

The hull he leaves for foreigners, partly burned
and shining in the depths. Downstairs
he entertains the sand with stories of his father

who loved birds and tattooed a lark on his arm.
The cave where at five he agreed
to show himself to little girls has grown.

It is no longer their expecting eyes making him alone.
It is not epiphanies of silent dancers
who sit down wondering if they are friends.

He confides to her that he has landed –
while she sleeps. The island is his own; the trucks
deposit workers at their stations in the fields;

men who never loved circle his fire;
the surf brushes a kitchenette where
the girl puts on the gas and waits.

He opens his hands and the lark is dead.
The sound of clapping shuts off; only
wind comes up the inlet,

whipping the flame,
finding holes in the forest,
blowing fine drifts over his legs.

Living with Strangers

On the way up to the room, my heart
folds three times and stops.
The women pass below,
naked branches in their hair,
going south, speaking of the long
overdue wind, the promises of strangers,
white air.

"The old boy, too bad, almost made it to his room."
They arrange me, laying down the silver
heads of Washington who was never afraid.
Winter in between the walls,
Mozart on the drums, I hear them leaving
for the movies, bowing, passing me on the stairs,
their feet scratching with the saints' claws.

I get up. Now I know I am living with strangers.
I climb to my room, my television:
A brilliant play comes on
where I am sitting in a lobby talking
to empty dark chairs. Turn the channel:
I have arrived in town embracing everyone. Two
young nuns mumbling "calm yourself"
take me back to the fourth grade.
Oh the murders I will commit
the rapes, the deliberate uselessness.
Without love, all things are possible.

I wave to a woman crossing the street.
She looks down, imagines I am dangerous.
The six o'clock news: I am convicted
of begging for attention.
I would like to recognize the people in the chairs.
"Poor old boy, took a nasty fall a day ago
thought he was dead."

I remember the rough stairs, the green doors
Margaret's black cigarettes, touching
knees on the way to a lake
the old room without any appalling
stillness.
White air.
The night watchman makes his rounds
in Winter, in the loneliness of mountain hotels
opens the box and slowly the chain
falls, dangles, the key shines in
moonlight. He holds it, blows
the frost from it, turns it in the clock.

What the Gulls Know

I see you standing at the edge of the waves.
Answering the gulls because they are content
to say the same thing. Because they are relentless
travelers in a region where monotony is the source
of life.

I see you trying to feel
as little of the pain as the salted air
allows. Trying not to be taken
by the white hands of the tide.
You have described

how the crowds wave from shore,
running up and back and pointing
to the unlucky one now caught
in the jaws of the beast.
You have described

the loneliness when he is pulled down.
The water again seamless.
Calm.
We speak obliquely of a drowning
as if it weren't your own.

So I hold you – because the skin listens
but does not speak – letting all that is hidden
remain. The name of the beast doesn't matter.
The gulls know that: Calling and calling,
as we do, to each other.

Elegy

"Men have a right to thank
God for their loneliness."
—James Wright

Who of us can keep death in sight.
You're gone, back into your river, James.
Back to Jenny now,
after waiting so long in this scarred,
echoing place.
And Jenny, dying young, could be generous:
Show you the right hand of loneliness.
There you are raising it, looking
through the fingers to see death
in every face.

But who can afford to keep death in sight.
A hardened snow in a hard light:
Those stinking bouquets for the girl
who started out with so much hope.
Not just the dead, but the murderers too,
they wanted something. They craved
at least the drifting moments of esteem
found on stoops of drinking men.

Snow settles in Ohio as a praise
on the levers, on the machines
of men walking in the early hours
to a job. The hands carry, the eyes
and lips say nothing
to those who are desperate for love.

Oh James.

Mine of the Lost Oak

Part one: The man who loved things when they were gone.

>The petals fell years ago,
>the earth returned to its place.
>The soft remarks of mourners
>rose and fell. Going out like
>sparks in a wolf-hemmed fire.

The last time he went mining
he heard his father's breath
laboring in sleep, deep and shallow.
In the pauses he foretold the slack
white hand, the hollow cheeks.

This time he remembers that his mother
took a beauty class on Tuesdays.
When he was in bed and she was gone,
his father went downstairs to smoke—
a basement that seemed then
infinitely far.

Always he dreaded the first creak
of steps, the descent, the silent house.
At a certain age, a child imagines
disappearance as death:
>Imagines death as stillness,
>the years vanish,
>the hand you hold vanishes.
You cannot get up in the dark
or shout.

He would like to find the vein,
the source of loneliness.

He loves his father now that he is gone.
He loves the details of memory.
Goodbye ... the anticipation clean,
dissociated from fear.
A bull night was expected.
In the mine his parakeet dies:
He continues to breathe the gas,
puts on the lovely melancholy vestment,
the moment that never changes.

His father is between breaths.
He loves a relationship
after death.

Part two: My car won't turn for home.

The runway was quiet.
I imagined that the plane had crashed;
that I was going on by habit;
I continued to descend the steps.

Light can be seen
catching the curtain on just one edge
as the room by contrast stiffens
in a rictus of late afternoon.

Almost transparent it is,
like the thin white blouse
on a murdered girl—almost transparent
and losing the last of the sun.

Now comes the rising murmur of dark
as if in finally knowing the wound
one could stop a death, or feeling it
thoroughly, undo this habit of insensitivity.

I see you from some distance
drilling redwood on the marks,
short of breath,
the last touches on the last
thing we built.

I'm not even afraid,
the sonance by then so commonplace.

It ends on a street like Taraval
with the green trolleys falling
in easy steps to the sea,
the storefronts snapping dark,
frame for the purple twilight gash
        thrumming
down at the end of the street.
My car won't turn for home,
keeps going on to where the shops
are less familiar,
and halts only at the beach.
The window is down to the roar
and above it a voice says:

"You don't mind at all
if I just get in?"
The lock's not down. He opens it.
"Chilly tonight."
And from the small duffel he pulls
his knife.

Part three: At the ends of the earth.

> The petals fell and were lost.
> Flicker-lit beasts
> who kept faithfully unheard
> bide just away from us.

I have always lived here in a dream,
making a family, then sending out word
that I have broken arms,
keeping everything the same:
The picture of the graveyard on my wall,
the desk of mementos.

I've stayed to walk a tilting plain
not watching the earth fall,
the conversation becoming more remote,
someone turning into stone,
a man saying volcanoes are the music of the dead
and finally sliding off, holding my
elbows in, stiffly treading where the ground once was.

There was an alley
at the ends of the earth.
Sweetpeas grew on trellises,
the sun was light green, bricks
the color of wounds.
An old man on his stool bowed:
"I have seen your life—
the screen of delicate paintings,
the boy fishing with a pole
that does not bend,
the women coming from behind a drapery,
stepping over the arched bridge
and around and disappearing back
into the drapery again.

"Your body in the rainbows of porcelain
is so thin, is so brittle.
You only know them as fingers
picking you up, putting you down
in museums they keep.
You will never know them,
the screen folds,
they climb the bridge,
the boy fishes after dark."
Then he gave me a picture of a field:

I saw three men cutting wheat,
keeping abreast of the slowest scythe,
reaping on the ends of the earth.
At first light I saw the vapors on the lake,
dogwood petals floating
in the wake of my hand,
the flowers of the dead not lost
the dead living in the field,
in the branches, the dead making the wheat grow.

At the ends of the earth
I could not dream,
the soil was black between the stems,
the old were wise because the dead
spoke in them.

Part four: What are we if not our father's eyes.

> He let me beat him once,
> the last checker gone; he said he played
> his best, put on his hat and took
> a business trip.
> I was elated.

You'd love to see New Hampshire turning.
I want to show you the red oaks.

I want to show you first-turning stands
like islands burning in a careless sea—
internally described as your thin ghost
would choose the elements of scene,
figure in a voiceless ground,
described in your very words.
What are we if not our father's eyes.

But the death in me
was partitioning off your own.

The trees here explain just enough of themselves
and we supply the rest: New Hampshire
cold like a gravity sucking north.
There's nothing seen, no attachment,
or object of fear
that isn't rumor filled with praise or harm,
that in the beginning you didn't lift up
to be seen.

Here is the list of particular values
to slap around our figments of a world:
      1. Safety; all downtown's an orphanage.
      2. Mountain is better than beach.
      3. Competence.
      4. Anger, like a thin mail, lies below
         the surface of things.
      5. Used cars that are cheap.
      6. Embrace, it is ending.
      7. Emotion be quiet: November quilts
         in their drawer.

I'd have a son to know you in myself
but he'd be alone here.

One hesitates to listen
to the road turning to moon,
cold, eager for a quick end.
The trick is a love
that disidentifies with death, ends,
and then recants the loyal despair:

Your legs white stems in the bed,
one learns it like an old
fortune with the date of each death.
Everything finally (in this
interpretation sieved from each possible fact)
finally gives out.
That was the seventh floor.

And I've worshipped since, in odd
cycles of fervor, the way
a man steadily retires.
An obsession kept, like a small
functional wound, to rub emotion out
and escalate surrender to a quilled idea.

It's time not to know the averaging emptiness,
all joining up like dust bowl caravans
of Fords & Chevrolets.
I want to show you these red oak
turning.

Part five: Mining

The character who makes his living
from exaggeration enters with a glass of port:
No one wants memory and the wolves' fire.

Do the dead linger, putting jewels in the eyes?
The past is concealed by the past,
mined to comfort and to regard

oneself in the proper light.
I give you the hand that has not been held,
I give you the boy in the bed: Myself or my father.

— — —

Places exist where a woman and man
on losing a child
plant an oak at the edge of their fields.

Out there
not much is said
because death has its good time.

Death has its good time
back at the house chatting,
welcoming as they draw up, friends.

Then Summer, Summer.
Three men come running to the lake
pushing their heads under crystalline water.

Table is set under the oak.
The murderer waits
for how big we have called the emptiness.

Toolbox

The living room gets dark.
In my hand is a postcard blank
save for the intake of breath
before hysterical laughter.

Today I fixed the porch, hammering
neat rows into the beams,
planned building a wardrobe and
sewed the ottoman.

It is easy to pass time, to run
circles around death,
getting large, large silver pliers
for all that needs tightening.

Another Person on the Train

We are
quiet in the chairs,
the light
flickering
through passing trees,
the light catching chrome
on cars
lost in meadows.

The plagues
sent to our fathers
are over, the exodus
over, we sway
together
through grade crossings
and switches,
letting go

like a breath
fogging the plate glass,
blurring flat
harvested fields,
the sudden
overgrowth of streams,
the phantom
destination.

So Long Muriel

Your invalided husband died, you took
a lover. Then in the auditoriums,
on regular nights, you started to dance:
The caller in that gaudy western shirt,
you turning toward the allemandes.

Except that you loved it, nothing
much is known. "Isn't life the shits,
Louise," are your last words to my mother.

Here we may begin the narcissistic eulogy
which hastens you away,
fluting safely to the cobra in
that complaining voice which dulls anxiety.
Or this
can be the milking of a distant death
for the private repertory stage
where the rare isotopes of rage and loss
are finally allowed their moments on:

Muriel, from your death I can enter a room
where I am very young. The window is open,
heather and the distant sounds of streetcars
coming in. Looking down, shadows
of clotheslines break a sunny lawn.
Two planting rows, two paths of concrete.
I have heard the garden talking about death,
the cool and hardly stirring air. I am
without the knowledge to describe the loneliness.
It comes as the first ruined dream.
But the feats of giving up are frightening
only if noticed.

I forget myself,
this has nothing to do with you.
Luncheon. Every one of the ladies came.
The good times hemorrhaged down your legs.

The Screen

On the newsreel,
my father said,
you can see the man reach
for a mooring line.
But in the wind the Zeppelin
starts to rise.
And he's holding on,
dangling higher,
until it's too late to let go.
And with the nose
still bucking he loses
hold, legs wild as if running
in air.

I imagined the shadow
passing the upturned faces.
As if auditioning for their own fall
much later at Salerno
or Guadalcanal. Or merely
upon opening a telegram.
My father's came in bed.
A slow descent
to the waiting fields –
lonely, hard as tarmac.
The fields taking him,
save the dust-light words
that made me.

I had always thought
the gravity is different now –
ancient deaths said
in a sentence, or not at all.
The past is a painted
screen where no life is felt,
the fear and loss
belonging only to ourselves.

But I keep seeing the man fall,
alone in the frame,
until each death
on its own far,
unreachable field

is real.

The Barn

Dirty straw, sheep
droppings. The animals
are gone. Gaps
where the boards have shrunk.
White, white webs.
Dust now
swirling in the streams
of light.

A woman
sings to a child
in another place.
Nothing matters.

Small Monologue

I know when he comes in, he said,
and when he uses the water.
I can tell
by his footsteps if he's depressed.
Underneath me he is thinking
about death.
We made love once
but our friendship was too precious

and he gave me six long-stem glasses
with a black rose in each.
He'd come up to watch TV tonight,
we would sit in bed touching,
and I would make witty remarks,
but lately he is having these
sexual flings because he thinks
I've been depending on him.

Lessons

In the schoolyard
some children become asphalt.
Some click lights off
in bathrooms where others
chipped and stained are toilets.

Class begins.
On the back wall
a picture of the Last Supper
has been redrawn showing
the messiah

as a hook-nose witch.
The nun goes into a rage.
At that moment
a child opens his desk,
leans in to become his own breath

that cannot be hit
that cannot be hit
that will remain
always empty
to the touch.

The Abiding

From here the city is fastened
in orange and gray,
the pines break ghost light.
The Bay becoming coal,

the emptiness this once a color,
an observable distance:
The cabled bridges and beyond
where ferries

carry the lips home
that have done their work,
that take comfort from the glass
and slight affection.

The wake fumes and gently
gently
(soundless here in the living room)
dies out.

Modoc Point

Chaparral shoves up between the rails.
I've come to find you in the weeds,
the swaying wires, a room
where the jump saws screamed.
Now in the silent August air

the mill town where you slept has turned
to shacks with old cars and a little lawn.
The roof has fallen on the store,
a few oaks spread in the sun.
My girl and boy won't leave the car.

So I tell how the snowlines blew across your bed
from cracks in the bunkhouse walls.
How you'd slip, poling the ice-capped logs,
into a freezing Klamath Lake. Stories
from that brief, unconscious season of your youth.

You went home in '38.
To my mother. And spoke from then on
through an interpreter: Your hands
lifting tools, turning pancakes,
drawing cross-sections on a napkin.

I could never find you there.
Wind from the north didn't touch
your death: The couch and tray,
the disease of sleep, a flickering light
from the Motorola.

The year you left, Lamm's Mill had 400 men.
A derelict dredge is moored
where the green chain hooked the floating logs.
The same clouds strut above the lake
as when you rowed out with your gun.

I came for what you saw: Cedar and fir
fixed in patches of light,
mallards keeping company
with decoys
out there beyond your blind.

In a Theater

In a theater
long after his death,
I sit with him.
He unbuttons his shirt
and shows me the scar;
knowing it will soon be opened
again. He's gone to the movies
with so little time to live.
I mingle in the gray
cells of his face.
Generations of men
return us our tears.
We surrender,
almost in relief
to the mesas of terror
and live there
not faking, not sleeping,
till he's gone.

Exactly Twenty Years

The distant Autumn light
comes down to touch your stone.
I am here to tell you
of these days you haven't lived.
About my children who were denied
your arms. My knees sink
in the soft, receiving ground.
The air stands relentlessly still.
Along the winding paths
between the stones
young joggers run.
Their bodies glisten.

Constantly you show me
how a man loves.

A Song of Otters

"Neither childhood nor future
grows any less in me..."
—Rilke

Once only
the gullied hills fall dark
above the fist-size stones
broken distantly by sharp lines of weed.

Once only
the cold Sierra slopes
turn green and breathe the shallow light
between wishbone trunks of birch.

We drift toward the empyrean,
the burning of memory,
with no way to hand it down.
So we must gather images.

The world sways, passes.
Once only
we become the foot and fly wheel
and the potter's last imperfect pressure

on a fluted jar.
The shadows intercede.
She knows but cannot recall
the Tigris at a wide bend, children bathing,

the sleep in which generations wait,
the mute gesture of a man
entering his tent,
a song of otters

in which life is lost
collecting and leaving everything behind
(a world saved by reflection)
without regret.

The Inheritance

Here is your desk, your chair;
your pen without its language.
Wind through the open casement
disturbs random pools of paper –
susurrant, full of rumor.

Death has taken your voice.
If you are to live
we now must speak for you:
Saying the same evil, the same good,
using the names you gave us.

Deeper in the room the lake starts.
Wind feathers it, making low
murmurings in water. And that gray sky,
telling the individual shapes of trees,
becomes at last something indifferent,

something to live for.

Miwok Trail

"We wonder whether these Californians [Miwok and others] had the most perfect adjustment to environment of any Indian tribe. Of all the U.S. Indians the Californians followed the simplest way of life. They were loosely organized, not over fond of fighting, and little given to roving habits....The whites despised them for all this, and hurried them toward extinction."

—Clark Wissler: *Indians of the United States*

1. Miwok trail cuts precisely in the hills,
the width of a dozer blade.
Their Spring delicacy, the clover, swells
in random concentrations through the fields.
Gullies, below us, flood with dark
which rises to the sun-fixed crests.

We are the last ones. To us
the hills speak only in a huge voice.
Night stirs the isolated oak
on Miwok trail.
Unknown dead see and go back to the world.
Their villages are mounds of shell & bone.

Reverence is the easy way. It's cool
and late, that's all we know.

2.   Necklaces jangle as they pound, acorns
        turn to meal, meal leached in the sand.
        The ball field is empty.
        Tule huts are damp with the rains.
        In the sweathouse, men dance in smoke.
        It's a question of favorable dreams:
        Quail for swiftness, Badger
        to help with the hunt.
        "Say nothing of it when the men refuse meat.
        Let them chant deer chants, and sweat.
        Speak and there will be bad luck."

        Women return from the mudflats,
        baskets dripping with sea water.
        The boys kill rabbits and birds.
        The shaman is dangerous if she learns
        to talk to owls.

        The women gamble at night –
        one hand holds the bones.
        Clams, mussels & oysters,
        shells dropped from men and women's hands,
        years in the same place,
        before our time.

3.   Mounds have been studied that were
thirty feet deep and three hundred around.
Across the Bay, one is the parking lot
for Spenger's Fish Grotto.

It's the past, and not our kin.
We're on Miwok trail – at the fork
and wooden bridge.
My spirit and yours that lie outside of us
have not been named.
Our dreams don't help.
The voice of lizard and cooling rock,
oak, wildflower, field mouse
is turned to one, is retained
in memory as, perhaps, our mood,
the greenness, the state of our bond.

Even the hawk, alone and
watching for movement, fills a story that
can't be heard.
And yet we have had our day.

Lucifer in the Resthome

He is retired now, fingers thin and picking lint
from newish corduroys. He is still angry
in the last days
of evil and good. As if it could have been stopped.

As if the kings could have said, "There is no
righteousness, only our need, only our power."

As if the saints could have said, "There is no
good, only this hard and arbitrary discipline
that yields sometimes a happy life."

As if we could say to Cain, "You are not evil,
only dangerous."

He is retired
in the last days of evil and good.
An early dusk milling in the living room
around the yellow circle of a reading lamp. He is
waiting for night, when finally in the quiet
cooling rooms
conscience is lost.
And finally the loneliness arrives
to force a passing sense of freedom.

Old men shuffle on the upper floor, the comforting
ablutions of lavatory, the opening of the made bed.
While Lucifer remembers the invention of good:
Think of a man, he used to say, trying to get
what he wants. He's got no weapon, no muscle.
Nobody gives it to him. So he calls what he wants
good. And not getting it he calls evil. Always
the need creates belief.

The man is afraid of loss, of men coveting his wealth,
of children leaving the clan, of lust that enflames
the lover who would take his wife.
He fears the foreign, the impulsive men
who are unrestrained by rules that keep him safe.
He calls it sin.

> *A good boy respects his father.*
> *A good boy is frugal.*
> *A good boy hoes the garden.*
> *But if he's willful, if he wastes, if he loves*
> *idleness, he has the devil in him.*

Lucifer rises. No one, he has found, can willingly
give up such power: To name things good or bad
according to desire. To raise a church upon the mere
ambition for survival.

He pulls the chain, and in the darkness finally
has his old man's bones, the clear and guiltless
pleasure of the waiting bed. He will watch television.

He sees:
> Newsclips of another march for peace.
> *Channel.*
> The all-night video preacher.
> *Channel.*
> A program on past braveries of the R.A.F.
> *Channel.*
> Two women sucking each other's breasts.

The Anteroom

You go to the window then,
in the Desert Moon Hotel,
through a room lit only by the amber
        of retreating light,
where table and dresser wash
forgiving shadows on the faintly lit back wall.

From the dark drowning there,
from the dark and lovely giving up,
you go with the merest interest
        to the dusky light.

Outside, the orange mesas rise to hold
a sloping field: A scratch of green
        where five horses stand.
Farther up the canyon it starves
into unconscious brown.

On the left a string
of Rio Grande coal cars. Engineless,
        cutting the field.
The wind strikes up a nervous
        passing music
on the outside of the glass.

You know then this is the anteroom
of death, safe for the losing
of last desires. The dresser still catches
        a pale fire. And suddenly the dead

the ones you knew
        who cared enough to come
are down there pointing
pointing to the landmarks.

The Geeks

Then these geeks came into the coffeehouse,
he said, jerking and fried the way they get
after too many trips, after years of drugs.
They ordered their wine.
I had mine and I watched:
Skinny, jerking in and out their cigarettes,
the white freckled arms correcting,
correcting what the nerves overdid.
It was easy to tell they loved each other.

Union Station

Blood stains in the clouds, the last light
silvering tracks west of the platform.
The train backs in carrying Autumn
from the prairies.
Doors open to the vestibules.
Attendants bend, placing the steps,
their shadows slurring into one, touching
the elbows of the frail.

The platform fills now,
heads and shoulders swaying
with the weight, faces
full of the chill, the rapid twilight,
the sight at the far end
of shelter.
Inside passengers receive the slight
immortality of high arched ceilings.

Greetings echo from the walls –
commingling to a single voice that tells
the latitude of all
the simple shame, the terror
hollowing the chest, saying
the prayers that have never been heard,
the names of all their dead,
telling the hunger to undress,

to be seen and finally taken in,
murmuring as if
it is all the same grief
dimming the high windows,
casting no specific shadow
on two strangers
who without reason or desire
suddenly embrace.

for Mary

Whatever Fortune
They Can Stand

A café
where women pass and go
among men sitting,
"Let me have and let me have,"
veins growing large and blue,
doing tricks with quarters
on the paper skin.

The gypsy comes around
to read palms,
each body rising slightly
from the chair when she sits down.

She says
whatever fortune they can stand.
If not the dreams, at least nightmares.

Sisyphus Goes to the Market

The cart,
heavy and trusted. The safety
of the burden that is completely known.
That careless arc
of boxes as they fall among the milk & loaves.

Eyes fix on the checkstand magazines,
the photographs
of those who have escaped the hill.

Now the tao of lifting. Bags lined
in the rear seat. Hot metal,
the ranting of the closed car.

Curtain light. Gray and thick
upon the chair and couch
and coffee table. No sound
except the rattling bags, the cupboards
opening and closing,
the meals being put away to feed
the infinite hunger.

The Dice

The flock sags on a power line.
Winter's throwing dice
for the weakened and the very young –
in each chilly shed
where men plane
boxes for their babies.
Let's say: Each last breath
is an argument for love.
While roads to the next house
go glittering and deaf in ice.

In my room,
which has no ceremonies for loss,
love itself will kill.
The lead bird takes off.
The rest explode from the wire,
empty and swaying.

Counting the Moon

Your death is a funny one.
Not practiced and done up.
Not a long argument
with boys who could drink all night.
Few people, you said, ever
have a good time,
and died at your window
nightly
counting the moon.

Each hour, then, had its moon.
Moon shifting in the shadow light,
the trees black
and casting blackness further out.

Then for once my death shows up.
He's hurt. He says, "For you
nothing is enough.
I have given you a hundred
things to love, the sweetness
of a passing world, a perfect end.
And you, who crave perfection,
have no time for any of it."

The Scrimshaw

The room, she says, is dark.
Unknown beyond the frail circumference
of the window light.

She sees the shadow of a cabinet –
glass doors – meant once for dishes
and empty now.

Her hands start to live
in the smooth grain of the shelves,
the dust becomes

a second skin on her palm. Dry.
Insensible. And then she finds
the scrimshaw:

An engraving of an open whaling boat
caught in the act of tipping.
Men with their arms flung out,

lances and harpoons falling
into the sea.
A humpback is ramming them.

The bone sky is white. Without memory.
Without feeling. She holds
the unexpected victory, wanting to begin

a risky celebration. A chance
for the hunted and pursued to cast
their vestal light into the room.

Parable of the Perfect Fields

An old man dies
and three sons come into their inheritance.
Each wants land,
a house set in perfect fields.
They leave town.

One never stops traveling. "My dream,"
he wrote, "is never matched. Not here,
not even here at this remotest place."
One finds what he can never love.
The letters turn petulant, complaining.

The last makes himself small
for the love of fields too flat, unbroken.
When the wind rises
at the end of two dry years,
the dry years and the wind
coming as was foretold
in their regular season, the soil goes
and he loses all that mattered to him.

For Whatever They Could Make

The porch shaded by madrone
is where life passes.
Geraniums beat in three redwood boxes:

The legacy of a man moving his
arm back and forth,
the nail pulsing deeper,
the hammer falling and after a while
the sound coming
as if reluctantly;

the noise given up by life,
the song that cannot be made
but comes of the will expanding.

The boxes are heavy with dirt.
I teach my lover
to put her hand
into the shape of his tools.
"The thoughts are gone,
only the act remains,"

as if, after all
the porch with three redwood boxes
is a place to sit,

as if the red-barked madrone
grew in the way of the sun, as
if all possible lives
pass through the mind
and are shavings
from tools passed on

for whatever they could make.

Trusting the Usual Deliverance

December wind
frags the street.
On the smokestacks
and high roofs
the angels are missing.

Only the wind remains
of hang-jowled
pulpit boys
doing their sacred barking,
believers nodding in the pews.

Now every corner has its own
currency and citizens.
A girl walks to school
between men whispering
the names of drugs. Each day

the girl can see her mother
in a board-and-care window.
Their signal:
If the window is open
she hasn't been drinking.

They'll visit that afternoon.
While the men sit
jackknifed in doorways,
trusting the usual deliverance,
nodding, nodding.

Her mother showed up
on her last birthday with a record
and left
looking up and down the street,
the wind swirling

in no particular direction.

The Three Angels

When it's dark,
when nothing at all moves in the house,
the three angels come:
One stands at the door,
one at the table, one at the bed.
They come to protect.
And though night may be heard
talking in a dog's bark, though
it talks from a rock clattering on pavement,
night cannot enter.
And the ladle and the pot remain
at the table.
And the bed is safe
from husky whispers of death.

Let us say there are three angels.
We can think of them and not disturb
their stations.
Let us lie down
as if they were keeping watch.
Sleeping early or late,
lying careless
in the flower of belief.

Begins a Pretty Death

Then the darkness running to meet me,
the fondling, relentless embrace.
In the backyard of childhood
birds get raucous in the fading pines,
whatever dwells in the underbrush
grows lonely and then evil, house lights
come on to loop in easy rows
around the hills, beckoning the faithful
workers herding home to sleep,
who'll soon again ride quietly downtown.

My body leaves me and I ascend
tetherless, without a sound, above
the rooftops and the steeples,
passed along by the colder & colder hands,
miles beyond the vapors and the planes
to where no witness hears the scream.
Then I know how I needed to prepare –
gathering the dreams
that no longer matter – so I can stand
to breathe the ice blue light of these stars.

The Valerie Hotel

River mist
pulls the bell at the back.
"Announcing death, Sir,
passing Rio Nido and Jenner tonight.
Is there a reply?"

Bundle the children inside.
Make of the guests
our deepest friends.

It's still our time.
Not yet the strength, but the dream
will wane:
The longed for, imaginary friend
must finally leave.
Laced fingers burn out of control.

Now, light we can't hold
backs to the French doors.
We gather for a meal, all guests,
all knowing the only room
that doesn't answer,
and serve around the heaping bowls.

Let us bend down then
in the Valerie Hotel
and wash the soil from each other,
and not be afraid of the loss
when one after one we leave,
and let death pass over.

Chances hammer the trees.
The nightmare of revealing too much
closes.
We visit one another's rooms,
sleeping in chairs till the windows
pink with early silhouette.
And death passes over.

Every Orphan Has a Suitcase

Tile that's arrogant
hexagonal
white
beneath the face
beaten
near the urinals.
Whiskey

on the bed table –
the day amber,
hothouse calm.
Memory a cloister
and a cell:
My father's slide rule
in its cracked
leather sheath.

Yosemite Poems

Requiem

White sparrows
                fly easily
ahead of the echoes
                fly easily
above stumbling horses
turning white on the trail.
                Steadily flying
through Indian snows
to a Summer of eyes: The roads
entomb a few caves
                where the acorns
were ground white in the granite
                where stalactites
grow over a fire-black ceiling
                when stone was enough
in the Indian snows
(white sparrows flying for echoes
that stay in the trees)
                where we listen to
granite, the seeping of water, ice
cutting boulders that fall on the echoes
of caves
where they nest; white sparrows
white horses
white flour
white mountains
white silence
white settlers.

Halfdome Turning Pink at Twilight

The face that accepts scars
rises above these ages of ice,
rises sheer
and faintly pink above the meadow
rustling with the work of fieldmice.

Here is the place you agreed to come
where nothing is wrong
nothing is human.

The granite becomes pink
as death comes for a day;
the day perfect in its dance and its disease,
perfect in love and love's denial,
ending in a meadow
of fern and grass and purple thistle.

No day left but a perfect lying down,
a fine desire to be kindly
and then cruel.
Oh fieldmouse, oh thistle,
I give you everything I am –
all love, all shame, all anger.
You will take it and give it back
clean and just the same.
And I will not have to despise myself again.

At the Fording Place

On the bank of Yosemite Creek
Gosse tells me stories of Napoleon and
        Marshall Ney.
We concentrate: His weekly visit
when the loneliness retards.

The water is nearly still and cold.
This pleasure would be enough to stay alive
if not for the sabotage of days
in between, the shards of conversation
in the store, an evening with its
white, ungiving moon.

Gosse makes circles in the river sand
showing battles lost and won:
The cannon were here and here Ney
was shot, somehow mounted and rode on.

Later we will drink
in the room where I have heard
my death speak in the scraping chair,
the ticking metal of the stove,
and where I think of boys
that hang from bone cut through
the breast. Renouncing fear
so at last and in the eyes of all
they will be men.

The water ripples past my ankles and down,
the rocks glitter, huge trellises
break in the labyrinth of one rose.
Ineffable dust falls and collects
on the dresser.

Gosse shows where the charge was blocked.

Long after dark he leaves.
Again I see that fording place where
people have been known to cross
above a deep cascade.
Someday when omnipotence grows thin,
the fear will not leave, and the visit
is long overdue: I will step in.
The rocks are slippery but the chance
becomes everything there is.

Wawona Hotel

We got up before light and drove
the still thoroughfares
and through the valley to Merced
before noon.
The August sun hated us: Every year
that river canyon left our city hands
wet, timid in the speeding blaze—
but Yosemite was the forest ahead.

Six hours at our best, before we made
the turn and stopped
and climbed the green stairs to register.
In a child's sight the building spread
around the lawns: Colonel and Mrs. Hall
married there in 1913, returning
every year for golf and limping silence.

That night the trees
were dark houses we had left.
Galen Clark built a station there
in 1864 and helped the stages run
to the foot of El Capitan,
and by the back cottages John Muir
planted four sequoias
which are watered every day.

I took the trees in me as ghosts
and watched the young girls at the pool.
Kissing my father and mother good night,
I went to the brass bed
and kissed the first woman I would know.
          The green death the black
          death I wanted to lie on the needles
          at night and shed the child
          and believe in the twilight
          and the dark cones, I wanted the
          breath of Autumn that knew.

In the morning my father and I golfed,
went back for lunch in the dining room;
the green day the black trees
in the bowl of night.
Colonel Hall played in front of us:
I imagined myself doing this at 85.
          Galen Clark was buried with cut
          glass around his grave
          and sequoias around the glass.
There must be a tree I would sleep under
breath I would hear
a religion in the forking branches
a green embrace.

We stayed two weeks every year.

John Muir Learned

I   John Muir learned
"The language of flood, storm
and the avalanche."

Uneasy stillness in white buttons
opening on breasts of denouement;

        the bed is carved
        where lovers lay near banks
        spilling a thin wilderness;
        perishing in a stranger's sleep
        and french horns deep within
        snow-laden boughs.

        There is the hotel,
        curtains flimsy as a hidden yawn
        but rest lingers on the drifts outside.

It is still there,
the tundra meadow cut
with creeks, contracting
when the head bursts out.

II   All at once we look up:
The trees bend and are taken,
the trail turns white.

We are replaced, replaced.

Part of a mountain weeps
but really it is projection,

an early thaw.

Robins collect dried needles
for their nests.
In a photograph
John Muir shows T.R. the sequoias.

Bayley's Joy

In 1875, Bayley, Washburn, and Muir
went south exploring the sequoias.
From Yosemite to Kings Canyon rim
they rise in isolated groves –
nothing small beneath them lives, just
shadow, giant trunks splitting the wind.
Bayley's joy, wrote Muir,
found expression then

in a kind of explosive Indian war whoop,
wild echoes driven from cliff to cliff.

They heard axes in those groves.
Muir watched a Big Tree
cut, the men prepare a butt section
for the Quaker Centennial.
Town dwellers paid their dollar to count the rings
marked "Columbus, Rome Falls, The Crucifixion,
Plato born 427 B.C."—awe disguised as
knowledge at so cheap a price.

"As well try to send a section
of the storms on which they feed."

Some Kind of Love Poem

It is dangerous to talk.
So we move between branches to the stream,
the statement of rocks
thrust from shadow
to the wet sun. Yes

and we lie down then
on hot granite;
the same rock where my father fished
pushing his thumb
through the gills
precisely cutting a spine.

It is dangerous to talk:
A thumb on the throat, a man
cutting the pain.
He climbs into the forest;
three fish,
they died so easily.

Witness

My father liked to fish.
A perfect stream, he said,
and stopped here in 1956.

The leaves still tremble above
Big Creek – shrill in the light,
gray in the shadows of pine.

Faint wind, dust in the saplings,
Chowchilla Road
dropping to a wooden bridge.

The sound of water
falling on water,
cold

where the sun touches
shadows of trout,
the water falling

down from the snowfields
over shoulders of granite.
Sand glitters with mica

in deep pools,
the surface a Janus
of shadow and light.

A perfect stream, said my father.
And now my daughter
is letting her line arc,

my son casts from the bridge.
I watch them,
knowing what changes.

For hours nothing comes
on the old road built
by Galen Clark.

I have Clark's picture,
second white man to see
the sequoias,

to see Muir Gorge –
he is serene, posed
to look into the middle distance,

        only a witness.

Edward Washburn Dresses Up

Fastidiously dressed
and bending thirty years at ledgers
in the back rooms of Wawona Hotel:
He was a soft touch for children
and never took a wife.
One thinks of him fussing,
making a hundred minute alterations
in collar and tie
on those two grand days:
The visits to Wawona of Roosevelt
and Taft.

> Dark comes for the continent,
> with a swagger walk, westward,
> comes here to the picture window
> on Twin Peaks.
>
> San Francisco stretches cold,
> hills heavy with the auguries
> of street light:
> A clear night to preside
> above the unattended deaths,
> darkness rising in the last
> casual goodbye.
> Tomorrow as the
> city smoke and vapors rise,
> their day begins;
> begins the roar
> of commerce seeking the exchange
> that does not require love.

By 1900 the hotel
was a small town. There were
stores, stables, a lumber mill –
all run by relatives and friends
of the Washburn brothers.
Uncle Ed remained correct,
a kindly father to
nephews and nieces left orphaned there.

They came into his stocks in 1911,
and the small inventory of personal
possessions: The stem winding gold
watch, gold cuff buttons,
his small diamond shirt stud.

Switchbacks

Granite chips support the trail's steep edge
at halfway where the heart goes dull.

I think you remember a shirtless boy
who lived in one of the Sierra camps
and worked the few warm months maintaining trails.
He cut his own way lithely over rocks

we labored on.
I was jealous of his thick arms,
his comfort,
his belonging to the trail itself.

We arrived at Merced Lake. You remember
the yellow tents circling a field;
in tall grass old men and women sitting,
carried here by trains of mules.

Somewhere on the switchbacks
we were not in love.
Birds flew out of your coat, but later
one-by-one came back to us.

Only the old arrived
without risking death.

For Martha

Full Moon

It's a cold night.
The air starts to listen
but there's no arrogance like a moon
lighting faint mists, leaving them
to speed giant shadows of pine.

Nothing here protects;
cold scores the bare flesh,
the moon can't be pleasured or denied.
The coat comes off, the shirt.
I'm facing the moon, among
stout trees, individual and dark.
In me, the old man is full, slowing
to stay here with what is alive.
I move out and into pools
where the shark light shines.

The Grove

High grass and lupine,
the light
sewn with shadows
of massive sequoia.

Barrett is gone.
I have the usual thought
that he can't see this,
that the dead

must leave beauty.
The wind
slides among the ragged
branches. Each wave

susurant as a final breath,
each wave
made out of stillness.
Ahead is the meadow

where Galen Clark,
consumptive,
failed miner & furniture maker,
built his windowless log cabin.

And lived to 96
guarding the trees as if

beauty
was the source of life.